S0-EAY-360

Friendship
and Other Poems

Marguerite de Angeli

Doubleday & Company, Inc.
Garden City, New York

Library of Congress Cataloging in Publication Data

De Angeli, Marguerite Lofft, 1889–
Friendship and other poems.

I. Title.
PS3507.E1684F7   811′54
ISBN: 0-385-15854-8
Library of Congress Catalog Card Number 79–6857
Text Copyright © 1981 by Marguerite de Angeli
Illustrations Copyright © 1936, 1940, 1942, 1946, 1953,
1963, 1964 by Marguerite de Angeli

I dedicate this book of verse to
Margaret Lesser Foster,
who was my editor and my friend
for many years.

M. de A.

About the Author

"Marguerite de Angeli, through the writing and illustration of her many books for children, has provided inspiration for a creative life to children and adults throughout the world;

". . . Through her own life, she exemplifies the highest quality of man's humaneness to man;

"She maintains her humility and sensitivity to beauty in people in spite of an impressive array of honors for her lasting contribution to the world of children's literature."

This apt tribute, inscribed to the author, accompanied Mrs. de Angeli's receipt of the Bergman Award for Outstanding Literary Achievement in Greater Philadelphia. Truly befitting such a *grande dame* of children's literature, the award expresses sentiments echoed by the many readers—young and old—who have become devoted De Angeli fans.

Mrs. de Angeli has written nearly thirty books since her first story appeared in 1936. Several books describe life in her hometown of Lapeer, Michigan, others recount the heritage of Philadelphia where she has lived for most of the last seventy-five years, and the rest span a myriad of topics. But all of her books exhibit personal warmth, wisdom, and a special insight into children's imaginations. A mother of five, grandmother of thirteen, and great-grandmother of three so far, the author has continually found her family to be a vital source of creative inspiration.

Mrs. de Angeli's many awards include a Newbery Award for THE DOOR IN THE WALL, Caldecott Honor Awards for YONIE WONDERNOSE and MARGUERITE DE ANGELI'S BOOK OF NURSERY AND MOTHER GOOSE RHYMES, the Regina Medal, and an honorary Doctor of Letters from Lehigh University. A most recent distinction was the proclamation of March 14, 1979, as "Marguerite de Angeli Day" in Michigan. Petitioning from an eighth-grade class in Lapeer prompted Governor William G. Milliken to make the special proclamation in honor of Mrs. de Angeli's ninetieth birthday.

Contents

Author's Note

These verses have been written over many years—whenever I feel I must express my joy in living, when friends are kind as they always are, when the clouds are especially lovely against the blue of the sky. As I grow older, I appreciate so many wonders that I took for granted when I was young, such as the marvel of tiny flowers that once I took for weeds, the exquisite perfection of a baby's hand, and oh, so much more!

For some years, my niece has urged me to try to have my verses published. Only lately have they been heard by friends or family who seem to have enjoyed them. I hope they express my thankfulness for friends and family, for health and happiness at a great age.

Friendship
and Other Poems

The Promise

Tonight, the clouds were dark and gray,
No sign of light nor clearing.
But then there came a band of red
And more and MORE appearing!
Till all across the sunset sky
Was crimson-glow so cheering!

The glory spread across the heav'n
And then I knew its meaning,
It seems there is a lesson here—
However dark the seeming,
However long the pain and fear
Light and Hope at last come gleaming!

Sunset

The beauty of the gold of sunset—
Glowing through my windowpane!
The city skyline—gray against it—
Silhouettes a weather vane

Gilds the crenellated towers
Of the churches here and there,
Intensifies the hue of flowers,
Makes thy lovely face more fair.

Lovely, too, the clouded sunset,
Shafts of gold thrust through the gray,
With benediction gently touches
Rooftops, treetops on its way.

Winter Trees

The wind in ceaseless moaning cries
Where stand the trees in nakedness,
Arms imploring surly skies
For warmth of spring and to be
Done with winter.

My heart in grateful loving sees Life
Flowing in its blessedness,
Like beckoning fingers of the trees
Asks warmth of Love and continuing care.

Twenty-sixth Street

Coming through my study window
On this dark and bitter day,
Rain and wind in constant moaning—
Even words that seem to say,
"Is there no place I may enter?
Is there no place I can stay?"

From the scattered chimneys standing
Plumes of smoke that drift away,
Old brown houses, mid-Victorian,
Silent stand, enduring cold,
Windows blank, in lonely guarding,
All within the house to hold.

Who lives *there,* I often wonder
What's the family in the fold?
Not a living soul is moving,
It's nearly zero, so I'm told.
A boy, scarf-bundled, comes a-sliding,
Turns the corner, and is gone.
I, to work returning, seek
The warmth of fireside and home.

Snow Fell

Snow fell,
Lay deeply,
Piled steeply.

Roof burdened,
Ice lanced,
Sun glanced.

Field pillowed,
Tree decked,
Twig flecked.

Branch laden,
Snow furred
Wind stirred.

Deer thicket,
Blue embraced
White traced.

Brook bound,
Ice clutched
Weed hutched.

Bird haunt
Quiet waiting
   Spring mating.

     Snow fell.

Valentine

Though the wind is bitter cold,
　　And I have your hand to hold,
Though I see you every day, and
　　You don't have much to say,
Yet, I know, or have a notion,
　　That I have your true devotion.
You have mine, as well you know,
　　Fair the weather, deep the snow.
And I'll be your Valentine
　　If you only will be mine!

Abiding Love

Of all the vows we mortals make
The one of "Wedding" takes the cake!
We promise then to undertake
To cleave to each, and to forsake
All others, save the Only One,
Whose hand and heart we keep, alone!
'Tis only Love that can atone
For slip or slight, or will condone
A sulky look or morning frown.

So—keep two bears within the house—
"Bear and Forbear" is the name,
These two beasts will devils tame,
And thrusting gibes will meet and maim.
("Abiding Love" is the other name.)

'Tis only Love will stand the test.
He liveth well who loveth best.

The Wedding

Where art thou, bird?
Hiding in the clotted leaves?
  I hear thy answer, stirred
Beyond the hill, where sunlight weaves
  A leafy pattern
On the unclipped grass.

  A flash of wings,
Thy jenny joins thee in a tree.
  I hear thee now. The round throat sings
Bursting with joy
  Thy jenny there to see.

  She yet escapes,
Sending forth her chirpy song
  Where the tool-shed window gapes,
But ere thy wings bear thee along
  She slips inside,
She warbles and she waits.

Being Grandma

Since these last, long months have passed,
More and more I seem to know
   That my "middle age" is past
And I'm really old at last!

   Think not it has made me sad—
Far away am I from that!
   Instead, I think of all I've had
Had? AM HAVING—that's not bad.

   First, there're all my children dear
Who grow in families year by year,
   Choosing mates I can't but love,
Each single one I'm thinking of!

They in turn have little ones,
Four at first and yet—no sons!
But time took care of seeming lack;
Soon, the laughing boys appeared.

First one, then two—how many more?
Each one as precious as the girls,
Carrying on the Family line
All sweet, all smart, and they are mine!

Chez Kuhn

In the morning, there isn't a sound!
  In fact, there is no one around.
    The coffee's not perking,
    And nobody's working,
And nothing to eat can be found!

By ten, there are sounds of awaking
  (A gargling sound Grandpa's making),
    Our Nina descends
    To make quick amends—
Eggs scramble, jam bramble, toast making.

Then, Nina is practicing Bach,
  Czerny, Mozart, and Liszt, by the clock.
    The metronome's clacking,
    The pump is a-whacking,
TV's sounding off on Bartók.

Our son-in-law's up in his room,
  To study and think, I presume.
      His typewriter's clicking
      And taking a licking,
The old text is meeting its doom.

Young David is scarcely at home.
  He's writing a scene (not a tome).
      He's hoping to be
      Not in sports, but TV,
And for such things, he may have to roam.

Guitar music's coming from Jeff,
  The G string is twanging A clef,
      Hank's horn is tootling
      While Grandmother's doodling
And Grandfather's turning quite deaf.

The China Figurine

This lovely month with woods alight
From blazing leaf and sunshine bright
   Brought you to us, dear Child of October,
A blessing and treasure, in gay mood or sober.

   Your birthday gift, which will not arrive
By train or by air (it is not alive),
   Awaits here your coming to carry it home.
(Its weight will not equal the weight of a tome.)

   'Twill be in a package that's easily carried;
By trainmen or planemen you will not be harried.
   It isn't a nightgown, a slip, book, or such—
In fact, you will think it's not anything much!

   It's not a tiara, a necklace, or zither—
It isn't worth getting yourself in a dither.
   It's little and brittle and easily broken,
Not a promise nor vow—but only a token
   Of love and affection from Father and Mother
Who think you a daughter beyond any other.

Maury's Forty-fourth Birthday

When I think back some forty years
    And see a curly-headed lad,
If I'd allow, there would be tears
    That boyhood's gone. Time makes me sad,
Except, with years, Time's made thee wise.
    Time's prerogative: to devise
Ways for continuing the race;
    Save lives and all inventive things
Find wives with loveliness of face
    And sons and what their growing brings.
Success, which hides behind Time's lag
    Consists in friends earned, work well done.
Can anything take place of these?
    Not all of money in a bag,
Nor all the gold of Croesus won.

Morning Light

How lovely is the dappled grass,
The circled chairs that encompass
    Grown-up talk and children's laughter
Remembered still the morning after.
    Lovely is the dappled grass!
Dewy morning's palimpsest.

On Peeling Apples

First, a sliver off the blossom end,
  Holding dry petals, my thoughts to send
To May, when pink and white
The fairy cup held bees' buzzing
And all of spring's delight.

The crimson, shining question mark of peel
  Curling in a twisting, spiral wheel
Frees the crispness of the apple's flesh,
  The fragrance of its sweet and sourness.

Round and round the glistening sphere
  To the tough stem standing there
In its deep hollow, dusty with summer sun and rain,
  Taking me to childhood,
  Bringing me back again.

Brief Moment

As I came down the moving stair
   And turned to go another flight,
A lovely child was standing there;
   I paused to see the charming sight.

Grave eyes met mine, and as I smiled
   A smile flashed back from lip and eye,
And friendship from the lovely child,
   An instant love. 'Twill never die.

To Edna

If I should tell the virtues all
That rest upon thy brow,
   Yet, height is there, in seeming, now
(I would not say that thou art tall),
   For all thy thought and gentleness
Is linked with wisdom and with grace—
   Each loving touch is a caress;
It shines in truth upon thy face,
   And shows in little acts of love,
Humble and sweet as mourning dove—
   Giving with heart and quiet mien
To all in near or broad domain.

   If fault there be, as in us all,
   I find in thee no fault at all!

Brotherhood
(The Day I Received the Regina Medal)

'Twas on a morning, such a morning bright,
Filled with sun and warmth and shining light
   And joy that overflowed because of joy to come.
One came and brought the breakfast to the room;
   Laid the golden cloth and on it spread
Silver and dishes and a plate for bread,
   Speaking to me gently all the while,
Saying how he'd reached that golden mile,
   Rising early in the dawning light,
Preparing dishes and the food to make all right,
   While others, dawdling, made no helpful move,
By idleness their lack of interest prove.

His willing service, long and gladly offered,
Yet many a scornful word and gesture suffered.
   But when our talk gave proof of his intent
To me and all mankind, a loving sacrament,
   With gracious and with pleasant praise
He took possession of my proffered book;
   Then, as if some understanding magic
Rent the veil of separation tragic,
   Two spirits, free of mortal hindrance dense
Of black or white or such encumbrance,
   Acknowledged in a sudden, quick annulment.
Love, the Universal, is complete fulfillment.

Friendship

Friendship is a silver ring.
Friendship is a lovely thing.
  Just begins and has no end.
Doesn't even need to send
  Messages on paper white.
Knows that all is well and right.
  Lives on thoughts and true affection.
Now and then has this objection:
  Time is short and meetings few.
So this brings my love to you.

He's Gone

I'll tell him—no—he's gone.
Or will he hear my wild heart's beating
At the cello's deep resounding tone?
At measured majesty of toccata,
Piano's broad bass, and the retreating
Triumphant, glorious staccato?
The elegy's solemn march, repeating
Sorrow's minor chords and major,
Showing Time's inevitable grace?
Light notes, like blossoms scattered,
Love and Life continue, keep their place.

I'll tell him—no—I cannot—he's gone.

Did he hear the music I have heard?
Was he there to see the things I've done?

I'd tell him, but 'twould be absurd
To think he'd hear.
Yet, his own hand played
The familiar melody, sweet sound.
Hears he voices that I cannot hear?
Disembodied angel voices clear?
The diapason of the heart's throb,
Measured sadness of the elegy;
Bliss of friendly voices, calling,
Old house, agape, with windows yawning,
Pieces of eight, artist in the barn,
Beloved child with friendship dawning,
Recorded voices, talking, chuckling,
Old friends to dine, to talk, rememb'ring—

I'll tell him all—Oh, no, he's gone.

Aging

My thoughts, these days, are too much occupied
   with death.
I think and think of how or when will Lethe
   Close eyes I love and steal away the breath,
Chill hands and lips and check the eager glance
   That welcomes me, and like a lance
Pierce to my inmost heart, because it cannot last.

But, I have today. Let winter's coldest blast
Strike when it must. That spirit bright
   Will far or near—or on some height—
Like the music of remembered years
   Speak through the mist, despite my tears.

Reprieve

When Death walks close
   And knocks on any door,
His grisly finger touches mine
   But hesitates a moment for
Time not spent and work undone.

   So turns, his somber garment rent
Where caught on ancient lock.
   Spares yet a winter's day,
   Turns back the clock
To daffodils unsprung
   To tales untold and songs unsung.

Lilacs

Plant me a lilac, dark and fragrant,
Over my resting place, under the sky,
Where the cool spring airs, caressing, vagrant,
Carry the perfume down where I lie.

Whether I be there, by earth enclosed,
   Or, spirit-light, hover near by,
The scent of the lilac will tell me, beloved,
   You love me still, e'en though I die.

May in Michigan

Away, away, across the field,
Lies a wealth of growing gold,
  Spread with lavish hand, and yielding
Springtime glory, braving cold;
  Thrusting forth, with Life renewing,
Filling hearts with praise, as viewing,
  ˙ We, the mortals, gazing, thankful
Field and meadow, sloping bankful;
  Glossy cowslip, damply bedded,
Dandelion, shaggy-headed,
  Quiet edict, gold and vernal,   ˙
Life and Love are both eternal.

  Certainly that Loving Spirit
Governs all that we inherit.

April

When daffodils and cowslips dance,
When tulips' pointed leaves advance,
  Hepatica in mauve and pink
Springs through leaf mold in the wood;
  The beaded dogwoods sway and prance
And lady's slipper thrusts its hood
     In silken sheen
     And golden green;
'Tis April, when the misty rain
Warms earth for flowers of May again.

London

If I should send you all the flowers,
Shaded greens, and winding ways,
 Grays and blues of clouds and showers,
Sudden sun in watery rays,
 The busyness of Piccadilly,
Tea and biscuits in the Mall,
 Art exhibits in the Gall'ry,
Guards in busbies standing tall—
 Then you'd have a bit of London—
Just a smidgen, that is all.

Surprise

No bird watcher am I, as such,
   Going on marches with a chosen few,
Up at dawn and scattering bright drops
   That hang on grasses and we call dew.

But there are those who come,
   As to a banquet spread,
To pick up bread and seeds upon the snow,
   And these I know.

Or by piercing sweet announcement—
   "I am here!" and "This is *mine!!*"—and go
By skips and swoops as wren or catbird fly
   Or bluejay's squawk or cardinal's liquid note,
Twitter of chickadee or sparrow's whited throat.

The hawk that sat upon the willow tree,
   The mourning doves whose sad refrain
Echoes through the early mist—
   These I know by sight.

Flashing flicker, mockingbird's scissored wing,
   "Come-drink-your-teeee-e!" the towhee's tiresome
      cry
On hot summer days when no bird sings;
   The cedar waxwing sleek, with eagle-hooded eye—
   I know these well by sound and sight.

But when the owl hoots in starless night,
   Shivering the heart at lovers' tryst,
Or, on display with other birds, all stuffed,
   He slowly *winks* and right before my eyes is
      LIVE—

I know him not, nor all his ways;
   Just to hear him is enough!

Tent Worms

I touch with flame the loathsome nest
Where budding almond leaves unfold,
   And writhing worms take dark night's rest,
   A silken canopy—to hold
A mass of wriggling ugliness.

   I shudder as they graze my hand,
'Reft of life and gossamer bed,
   Then quickly move from where I stand
To pluck a worm from off my head.

   I brush another from my face.
Yet, could I with consummate skill
   Or any effort of my will
Weave such a tent of gauzy lace
   For my children's dwelling place?

Wonder

The hand that holds the ocean wild
   And lifts the rocky islands high,
Sets the stars in constellation,
   Secures the land beneath the sky,
Feeds the birds that skim the waters,
   Nests them on the rocky ledges,
Holds the pattern of their flying,
   Guides their passage in migration—
Lifts the heart in adoration.

   Awesome wonder fills the soul
At Creation's mighty grandeur
   And the infinitely small!

Autumn Morning

Morning wakes, a catbird sings,
   Doves rise up on whistling wings,
Dewy roses soft unfold,
   Falling leaf is purest gold.

Rocky outcrop, green or gray,
   Where the beaded branches sway,
Stony path on twiggy sod,
   Misty hills—all speak of God.

October Day

What bright angel—winging
On his appointed round—
    Set clouds afloat in the heaven?
Was it Gabriel or Michael?
    Or one of six or seven?
Who, with angel finger light
    Traced each feathery form
On swift and luminous flight?

The airy patterns are clear
Against the cerulean blue,
    Yet, moment by moment they move
And take on patterns anew.

One wonders at the heavenly sight
And lifts one's heart to a heavenly height.

Transcendence

When comes my time to leave this lovely Vale
　　Let me not give pain to those I love,
But gently slip away through that dark Dale
　　Where harmonies in a garden move
And draw me on to flowers fragrant, bright—
　　Where loved ones wait, all shadowy, but real,
Loved ones long gone beyond my ken and sight—
No moon, no sun their separate selves reveal
　　But God's own lovely light floods all!
And then I know all's well and I am Home again.

De Angeli, Marguer-
ite Lofft

Friendship and
other poems

29882